Thou Shalt Not Kill

Unless Otherwise Instructed

T0347279

Thou Shalt Not Kill

Unless Otherwise Instructed

[Poems and Stories]

Mike Sharpe

Routledge
Taylor & Francis Group

LONDON AND NEW YORK

First published 2005 by M.E. Sharpe

Published 2015 by Routledge
2 Park Square, Milton Park, Abingdon, Oxon OX14 4RN
711 Third Avenue, New York, NY 10017, USA

Routledge is an imprint of the Taylor & Francis Group, an informa business

Library of Congress Cataloging-in-Publication Data

Sharpe, Myron E.
  Thou shalt not kill unless otherwise instructed : poems and stories / Mike Sharpe.
    p. cm.
  ISBN 0-7656-1722-6 (pbk. : alk. paper)
  1. Iraq War, 2003--Literary collections. 2. Current events--Literary collections. I. Title.
PS3619.H35665T48 2005
818'.609--dc22   2005014240

ISBN 13: 9780765617224 (pbk)

To my wife Carole.

To my children,
Susanna, Matthew, Elisabeth, and Hana.

The Noble Duke of York
He had ten thousand men
He marched them up the hill
And marched them down again.

Contents

IV The New Traffic Rules

V Earlier Drafts

I *The Twin Towers*

The Twin Towers

I speak of the twin towers of memory still standing in
memory present in absence present in images I search for the
twin towers in images to fill a heart-aching absence

Dates before the towers and after the towers America before
the towers and after the towers innocence before the towers
and after the towers safety before the towers and after the
towers fear before the towers and after the towers disaster
before and after

The planes coming in colliding with the towers repeat
colliding with the towers television repeats colliding with
the towers wounded at 8:46:31 wounded again at 9:02:59
wounded never to recover anguish radiating from the twin
towers fireball fireball repeated the towers stabbed over
and over

People escaping people burned people jumping stairwells
blocked firemen going in the smell of burning flesh
confusion smoke dust clouds people running terrified
faces cloths over noses mouths buildings coming down
straight down collapsing straight down we are terrified to
see them horrified to see them debris on the ground gaping
nothingness but the twin towers remain standing in images
in our minds

The goodbyes on cell phones the lucky ones late to work or
sick at home or delayed by early meetings neighbors who
didn't come home the confused the bereaved

The nineteen murderers learning to fly in order to die people
on the planes men women babies false calm in the buildings
miscommunications heroism of firemen ignorance ineptness
wrong plans time to get out for some but they didn't know

The shock of the world the world united speeches meetings
what happened what caused it why weren't we ready
why wasn't it stopped two ghost limbs still aching

Then monumental madness a giant strikes wildly wrongly
kills more than were killed destroys more than was destroyed
exacts pain for pain exacts sadness for sadness the world is
aghast at a meaningless crusade jihad against jihad

We send a demanding message but we send the message to
the wrong address we march out to the wrong destination
we exchange our dead for their dead the world shrinks back
from new holy wars oh towers of our remembrance how
wrong to be reduced to hubris and lies

Nightmares

The twins woke up suddenly, suddenly.
Suddenly the twins woke up.
I had a terrible dream –
I had a terrible dream.
I dreamed about a twisted Daddy –
I dreamed about a twisted Daddy.

How many kids did you kill today, Daddy –
How many kids did you kill today?
How many moms bled today, Daddy –
How many moms bled today?

You fry for killing one man, Daddy.
You fry you fry you fry.
What about ten thousand, Daddy –
How about ten thousand?
How about that, Daddy?

We hate your smug face, Daddy –
We hate your smug face.
We hate your sick mouth, Daddy –
We hate your sick mouth.
We hate your fake Texas boots.
We hate you, Daddy.
We hate you hate you hate you.

Have you taken war for a wife –
Have you taken war for a wife?
What about Mother –
What about our Mother?
Mother Mother Mother –
Daddy war lover?

You're not unlike someone with a little moustache, Daddy –
You're not unlike somebody with a little moustache.
You, instead, have a little scowl –
You have a little scowl.
With a God bless and a God bless and a God bless.
And so cocky cocky cocky.

You think you have the whole world in your hands, don't you –
You think you have the world in your hands.
Just like God just like God just like God.
You're not God, Daddy.
You're not God.
Little man little man little man.
You bastard.
You're a killer a killer a killer.

The Capacious Tent

You went to the capacious tent
For a burger and a Coke.
We honor you for who you are.

Soldier, you didn't think this through.
You walked into a trap.
We honor you.

The trap was set here not there.
Orders sometimes must be questioned.
We honor you.

You believed what you were told.
You are too trusting.
All honor to you.

Why didn't the president send his daughters, you ask.
What kind of fool do you think he is?
You are a hero.

Not so foolish as your father
Nor his daughters as foolish as you.
It is you we honor.

If you give your life for your country
Shouldn't you get something in return?
You served honorably.

You, soldier, entered the tent of death –
The cost of being wrong.
Still, we honor you.

It's Hard

A boy was coming toward me.
His hand was in his pocket.
I shot him.
He had nothing in his pocket but candy.
It's hard to kill a boy.

An old woman was coming toward me.
Her hand was in her coat.
I shot her.
She had nothing in her pocket but a white kerchief.
It's hard to kill an old woman.

A car was coming toward me.
The car was full of people.
I shot them.
The car had nothing in it but a family.
It's hard to kill a family.

The President Delivers His Second Inaugural Address, January 20, 2005. The Children of the World Address the President. The President Does Not Respond.

The best hope for peace in the world is the expansion of freedom in the world.

> *Five million children are dying of hunger every year. Can you help us?*

. . . every man and woman on this earth has rights, and dignity, and matchless value . . .

> *The available food in the world is enough.*

. . . we have proclaimed the imperative of self-government . . .

> *Two million children have AIDS or HIV.*

. . . seek and support the growth of democratic governments . . .

> *And AIDS has orphaned fifteen million.*

. . . the ultimate goal of ending tyranny in our world.

> *Six hundred and forty million children have no*
> *adequate shelter*
> *Five hundred million have no sanitation*
> *Four hundred million have no access to safe water*
> *Two hundred and seventy million have no access to health care*
> *One hundred and forty million have no schools*
> *Ninety million are starving*

. . . when the soul of a nation finally speaks . . .

Not immunized, dying each day – eighty thousand
Dying from diarrhea each day – seven thousand
Dying from pneumonia each day – six thousand

. . . attain their own freedom . . .

More than half the children of the world – over a billion
– suffer extreme deprivation.

. . . America's influence is considerable . . .

The cost of solving children's health care problems – two-
and-a-half billion.

The moral choice is between oppression, which is always
wrong, and freedom, which is always right.

The United States is last in its contributions among
twenty-two industrialized nations.

. . . the decent treatment of their own people . . .

Twenty-two percent of American children live in poverty.

. . . the power of our ideals.

The United States spends less than two-tenths of one
percent of its gross national product on foreign aid but the
United Nations asks for seven-tenths of one percent.

All who live in tyranny and hopelessness can know the
United States will not ignore your oppression or excuse your
oppressors.

Eleven million children will die needlessly this year.

God moves and chooses as he will.

> *The cost of the war in Iraq: two-hundred billion so far;*
> *The cost of the US military: running four-hundred-and-seventy billion;*
> *The cost of fighting world poverty: forty to seventy billion in the coming years.*

. . . history has a visible direction . . .

> *Please, sir. More help.*

America, in this young century, proclaims liberty throughout all the world and to all the inhabitants thereof.

> *First we must eat.*
> *First we must drink.*
> *First we must heal.*

. . . we are ready for the greatest achievement in the history of freedom.

> *Or we will die.*
> *Or we will die.*
> *Or we will die.*

Elegy for American Soldiers
Killed in Iraq

Roberto Abad Brandon Adams Daniel Amaya
Levi Angell Todd Bates Trevor Blumberg
Adam Brooks John Brown Joseph Camara

Have you been thinking of a monument yet?
We need another wall on which to inscribe these names.

Jessica Cawvey Brian Cutter Torey Dantzler
Mark Engel George Fernandez Benjamin Freeman
Dimitrios Garriel Joseph Garyantes David Goldberg

Let us gather up the names and inscribe them on a wall.
Let us make another wall.

Hans Gukeisin Kimberly Hampton Keicia Hines
Leslie Jackson Brian Kennedy Joshua Ladd
Roger Ling Joseph Maglione Don McMahan

This wall is between us and them.

Jesus Medellin Adam Mooney Shawna Morrison
Paul Nakamura Ramon Ojeda Cody Orr
Rafael Peralta Kelley Prewitt Ryan Reed

It is not sweet and fine for your name to be inscribed on
this wall.

Scott Rose Isela Rubalcava Michael Scarborough
Uday Singh Antoine Smith Paul Storino
Sharon Swartworth . . .

We need a wall where we can go and contemplate what we have done.

Go to this wall to read the names.

Leave space on the wall.

Eight Days in Falluja

Two marines inched upward inside a dark minaret.
Gunshots came from the top of the tower.
A marine named Miller lay mortally wounded in the face.
The second marine fell backward down the steps.
Several others made four attempts to rescue Miller against
gunfire from the tower. Finally Miller's body was brought down.

Bravo Company had one-hundred-and-fifty marines.
Each marine carried a seventy-five pound pack.
In eight days they suffered thirty-six casualties.
Six of the marines died.

A marine named Knospler entered a darkened house.
A hand grenade blew off part of his jaw.
Several marines dragged him out of the house.

Forty-five marines dashed across Forty-Second Street.
They ran into crossfire.
Five fell down bleeding.
A marine named Wells lay dead on the roadside.

Ziolkowski was a sniper on a rooftop.
He waited for hours at a time.
He killed three men in one day.
Snipers on the other rooftops "are trying to take us out."
He removed his helmet to get a better look.
A bullet knocked Ziolkowski backward onto the roof.
He was hit in the head and he died.

The marines were very young. They wanted to get out of small towns. They wanted adventure. They wanted to shoot people.

Bravo First Platoon went down a dark alley. They met insurgents coming the other way disguised as Iraqi National Guard. The insurgents opened fire. A marine named Anderson lay dead. The rest of the platoon pulled out. All at once an ambush, flares, gunfire, and screaming. The men got rattled and argued. Lieutenant Eckert tried to take charge. Captain Omohundra had to intervene. The unit held out. "Damn it, get moving. Keep a sharp eye. We ain't done with this war yet."

Proof of Torture

The administration practices torture.

Fear of losing arms, legs, or being paralyzed, burned, or
blinded.
Fear of death in war.

Losing arms, legs, or being paralyzed, burned, or blinded.
Being torn apart and dying.

Ripping flesh and blood.
Devastating cities.

Parents waiting for news.
Children waiting for news.
Brothers, sisters, and friends waiting for news.

Parents receiving official notice.
Children receiving official notice.
Brothers, sisters, and friends receiving official notice.

The loss of sights and sounds and smells and tastes and
touches.
The loss of love and children and work and rest.
The loss of fifty or sixty years.

Coming home and never forgetting.

A war founded on a lie.
Torture to avenge torture.

Silence.

Proud to Be American

If we remained children,
Fairy tales would do.
But fairy tales are not suitable for grown-ups.

> Our history is one long story of noble exploits.
> God told us to do what we're doing.
> We are wholly altruistic in our actions.
> We are blessed to live in the greatest country in the world.

As long as children are children, these stories might do.
But now that we're grown-ups, a little modesty is in order.
We haven't quite climbed to the pinnacle of perfection.

When love and mercy unclose our eyes,
When the some-day America keeps its promises,
Then maybe a little modest pride will be justified.

Iraqi Prayer

Eventually they will go away
Let us hasten the time
Each in his own way

We will deal with the assassins
Let us hasten the time
Each in his own way

May we live
Or not
As God wills

Tsunami

Let us add to mankind's woes
the lack of an early warning system
for tsunamis
around the globe.

Not since the war in Iraq
have we seen devastation like this
where an early warning system was also –
absent.

I Saw This

I lived on the edge of holocausts and wars.
By mere chance I was spared from pestilence and starvation.
I came near but not within the grasp of dictators and torturers.
The poor lived around me but not too close.
For no particular reason I was spared the wretchedness of prison.
I had work when others were consumed by despair.
I had rooms and a garden while others suffered humiliation.
I read the news of massacres at breakfast in a comfortable chair.

The good people took little pleasures between catastrophes.
They took little pleasures during catastrophes that happened
somewhere else.
Leaders were the most innocent of all.
They knew no other way.

I never thought it had to be this way.
I always believed there was another way.
I merely report what I saw.

II *The War Crimes Trial of George W. Bush*

Who's Winning?

Our side is winning.
We lost about eighteen hundred men and women.
I mean they were killed.
A small price to pay, everything considered.

Of course every death is unfortunate.
But the other side lost forty or fifty thousand not counting
civilians.
I'm really sorry about the civilians.
But whose fault is it? Not mine.

Of course hostilities mean that some folks are going to be
wounded – lose arms, legs, eyes, and other body parts.
I feel bad about that but these guys are resilient and adjust
back in civilian life.

The other side has wounded folks likewise, as you know. I
feel bad about that too.
How many? Maybe half a million – you'll have to ask the
Red Cross or the Red Crescent or whatever. We don't look in
every ditch.

Here's the bottom line: We all know the spread of freedom
and democracy doesn't come cheap.
A tyrant was overthrown and the people will not suffer death
and maiming at his hands any longer.

My detractors say we destroyed a country for nothing and turned a billion people against us. Well, you can't please everybody.

Believe me, we'll win over hearts and minds by showing them who we really are.

Mark my words. God bless.

The President Recognizes
Three Public Servants

The chief of the Central Intelligence Agency,
an honorable man who unfortunately was unaware
that terrorists might attack,
received the Presidential Medal of Honor
for good intentions.

The four star general in charge,
an honorable man who regrettably
didn't summon enough troops,
also received the Medal of Honor for a noble effort.

The proconsul in occupied territory,
an honorable man who sadly failed to plan
for the aftermath of war, was third to receive the Medal.
He too did the best he could.

You say you have a problem with this?
Lives were expended recklessly, you say?

Well, show me anything in life that goes exactly as planned.
The President honors men who stand up for our ideals
and rejects petty criticism.

The Indictment of Saddam Hussein

May it please the court

The case against Saddam Hussein for crimes against
humanity is lengthy

In addition to mass murder before the war

He caused the President of the United States to believe
that he had Weapons of Mass Destruction
Or wanted to have Weapons of Mass Destruction

He caused the President of the United States to believe
that he sheltered terrorists
Or wanted to shelter terrorists

He caused the President of the United States to order
the invasion of Iraq
At great cost in human lives

And the destruction of Iraq
and the insurgency against the forces of freedom
And democracy

And the enmity of Arabs and Europeans and Asians and
Africans and Latin Americans against said president

May it please the court
It will be proven –

All these crimes and more
Are on the head of Saddam Hussein

The War Crimes Trial of George W. Bush

Presiding judge: Read the indictment.

Prosecuting attorney: We charge George W. Bush with war crimes as follows:

He accused Saddam Hussein of possessing weapons of mass destruction and he didn't have them.

He accused Saddam Hussein of complicity with the terrorists who struck the United States but he was not in complicity.

He launched a war against Iraq, killed and wounded innocent men, women, and children, and ravaged the country.

Presiding judge: How does the defendant plead?

Defense attorney: Not guilty, your honor, on the following grounds:

It was reasonable for the president to assume that Saddam Hussein was also a reasonable person.

A reasonable person in Saddam Hussein's position would have weapons of mass destruction.

A reasonable person in Saddam Hussein's position would have links with the terrorists who attacked the United States.

A reasonable person in Saddam Hussein's position would realize that it was useless to resist the US armed forces and would have saved the Iraqi people from a devastating war.

Therefore, since George W. Bush is a reasonable person who made reasonable assumptions and acted on those reasonable assumptions, he is not guilty of war crimes.

Presiding judge: The court will adjourn and consider the case.

Later.

Presiding judge: The court has reached a verdict. In view of the facts that it was reasonable for George W. Bush to assume that Saddam Hussein was reasonable, and that a reasonable person in his position would have weapons of mass destruction, ties to terrorists, and a desire to spare Iraqis death and destruction at the hands of the US military: In view of all these facts, we find President George W. Bush not guilty.

Support Our Troops

Support our troops by displaying bumper stickers
Support our troops by giving parties
Support our troops by going shopping
Support our troops by standing on the sidelines
Support our troops by keeping your mouth shut

III *Never Again*

His Heart Was Heavy

Christ slipped back into town.
His heart was heavy with what he saw.
His heart was heavy with what he heard.

Christ felt that irreparable damage had been done.
His heart was heavy with what he saw.
His heart was heavy with what he heard.

Christ heard a great sigh and a great moan.
His heart was heavy with what he saw.
His heart was heavy with what he heard.

Christ perceived a burden he could not lift.
His heart was heavy with what he saw.
His heart was heavy with what he heard.

Christ heard a mob approaching.
Christ saw a mob approaching.
And the mob took him roughly.
And the mob took him as a man condemned.

And they crucified him.
And they crucified him.
He never said a mumbling word.
He never said a mumbling word.
He just bowed down his head and died.
He just bowed down his head and died.

Heartbreak House

We have books.
We read The New York Times.
We watch CNN.
What can we do?

We talk at the table.
We invite friends.
We express dismay.
What can we do?

We have difficulty eating.
We have difficulty sleeping.
We have difficulty getting through the day.
What can we do?

We will not go along.
We are sorry for those who will.
We talk incessantly.
What can we do?

The Condemned Protests the Bright and Shining Future

We are killing you because the end justifies the means, said the executioner.

How do you know that you will achieve the end, said the condemned.

The end is bright and shining, said the executioner.

I fervently believe that we will achieve the end, said the executioner.

The end is compelling beyond all other considerations, said the executioner.

Not to me, said the condemned.

War

The bullet hit him.
He died.

The bullet missed him.
He married, had children,
Worked, traveled, watched TV, danced, read.
Then he died.

The General

Napoleon, retreating from Moscow,
Kicked a French corpse and said,
Thousands of these are conceived in Paris every night.

The Unnecessary War

The unnecessary war
Brought unnecessary death
Unnecessary ruin
Unnecessary hatred
Unnecessary fear
Unnecessary madness
And was conceived by an unnecessary leader
As an unnecessary mission
Not accomplished.

The Mobilization Orders

The mobilization orders were drawn up
and then the reasons for the orders were drawn up.

Lord Acton Forgets

Lord Acton forgets the other side of the equation:

Powerlessness corrupts. Absolute powerlessness corrupts absolutely.

On Evil

Some men are born to be evil
    — a very small number

Some men achieve evil by their own exertions
    — a much larger number

Some men have evil ways thrust upon them
    — most of the rest of us

Some men cannot be evil
    — not too many

Some women are born to be evil
    — about the same number as men

Some women achieve evil by their own exertions
    — not as many as men

Some women have evil ways thrust upon them
    — not nearly as many as men

Some women cannot be evil
    — probably the same number as men

Never Again. Never Again. Never Again.

The general spoke.

The general said: *It's fun to shoot people.*
It's fun to fight.
It's a hell of a hoot.

It gives you a rush, doesn't it, general? Makes you feel fully alive, nerves all a-tingle. The other man-woman-child lies on the ground or in the bush fully dead.

What shall we do with the general with the lethal addiction? The general who likes to shoot people? The general surrounded by young warriors who drink the anodyne? Who kill. Who see the killing. Who see the dead. Who come home dead inside.

I like brawling, said the general.
I like killing.
What shall we do with the general who likes to kill?

They (the generals, the dictators, the presidents, the terrorists) like to kill people.

Then we said, Never again!

They liked to kill Armenians.
They liked to kill Jews.
They liked to kill Vietnamese.
They liked to kill Cambodians.

They liked to kill Bosnians.
They liked to kill Rwandans.
They liked to kill people of Darfur.
They liked to kill Iraqis.
They liked to kill Americans.

We said Never again! Never again! Never again!

You and I (Who else? There is no one else) are going to decide who wins this deadly contest, the murder-maddened with their premeditated Murder again, Murder again, Murder again, or the death-maddened with our own premeditated Never again! Never again! Never again!

If you are in the path of war, slogans might not get your attention. You wouldn't be thinking about slogans. You would be thinking about staying alive. It doesn't pay to know too much about this predicament. You might worry. If you can't put yourself in that man's place or that woman's place or that child's place, what will you do when the intended victim pulls at your sleeve and says, "Help me"? Can you help? Will it be too late?

It will be too late. I'm afraid it will be too late.
If we decide against war, why do we wait? Waiting is too dangerous. If we are in the path of war, it will be too late. Are we waiting for the conditions to be right? They are right when we decide they are right.

Beware the general. The general (and the dictators, the presidents, the terrorists) is very persuasive about the liberating war to come. Beware again, beware again, beware again. Beware the intoxicant. Beware the anodyne. Beware the allure of procrastination. Beware, we are breaking a primeval addiction. Beware, let the doctors minister to the general. Beware, let the general slowly detoxify in sanatoria.

If we all want to end ten thousand years of war, isn't there power in knowing that? Get on the cell phone. Get on the Internet. Do you want to wait another ten thousand years?

* * * *

When wars are past, when the evening star next sets in the west, when the thrush next sings its reedy song, when lilacs next in the dooryard bloom, we will think of the fallen. When wars are past, we will think of a new world, the old never to return, never to be forgotten.

Two Conversations

I

Thou shalt not kill, said Allah to Osama bin Laden.
I hear sighs and cries; where is thy mercy to men and women?

Replied Osama bin Laden: The learned have said: To everything
there is a season, there is a time to kill and a time to heal. Thus
have the learned said.

The learned may say. But ye shall be rewarded for aught but what ye
have done. He that rolleth a stone, it will return upon him.

You, Allah, are distant, far removed from the affairs of men.
How can men be pure while the earth is vile?

Woe unto them that call evil good and good evil, Osama bin Laden.

Hath not Saul slain his thousands and David his ten thousands?

They have done what they have done. My thoughts are not your
thoughts, neither are your ways my way.

I do not walk the earth exultantly but only for Allah.

The words of your mouth are smoother than butter, but war is
in your heart.

You are remote, Allah, from the affairs of men, and Saul has slain
his thousands and David his ten thousands.

The works of unbelievers are a mirage in a spacious plain. So I have said.

We must kill while evil walks the earth. I do not kill exultantly.

Osama bin Laden, remember that pride goeth before destruction, and an haughty spirit before a fall.

Men cannot be pure while the earth is vile, Allah, or the vile will rule the earth.

Remember, Osama bin Laden, whoso diggeth a pit shall fall therein: and he that rolleth a stone, it will return upon him.

You are far from the affairs of men, Allah. Men cry peace but there is no peace.

My thoughts are not your thoughts, neither are your ways my way. Where wast thou, Osama bin Laden, when I laid the foundations of the earth?

II

Thou shalt not kill, said God to George W. Bush. I hear sighs and cries; where is thy mercy to men and women?

Replied George W. Bush: The learned have said: To everything there is a season, there is a time to kill and a time to heal. Thus have the learned said.

The learned may say. But ye shall be rewarded for aught but what ye have done. He that rolleth a stone, it will return upon him.

You, God, are a distant God, far removed from the affairs of men. How can men be pure while the earth is vile?

Woe unto them that call evil good and good evil, George W. Bush.

Hath not Saul slain his thousands and David his ten thousands?

They have done what they have done. My thoughts are not your thoughts, neither are your ways my way.

I do not walk the earth exultantly but only for God.

The words of your mouth are smoother than butter, but war is in your heart.

You are remote, God, from the affairs of men, and Saul has slain his thousands and David his ten thousands.

The works of unbelievers are a mirage in a spacious plain. So I have said.

We must kill while evil walks the earth. I do not kill exultantly.

George W. Bush, remember that pride goeth before destruction, and an haughty spirit before a fall.

Men cannot be pure while the earth is vile, oh God, or the vile will rule the earth.

Remember, George W. Bush, whoso diggeth a pit shall fall therein: and he that rolleth a stone, it will return upon him.

You are far from the affairs of men, oh God. Men cry peace but there is no peace.

My thoughts are not your thoughts, neither are your ways my way. Where wast thou, George W. Bush, when I laid the foundations of the earth?

Thou Shalt Not Kill

Thou shalt not kill, said God.
I'm in agreement, said Osama bin Laden
I'm also in agreement, said George W. Bush.

Then why are you killing people? asked God.
I assumed there were exceptions, said Osama bin Laden.
I also assumed there were exceptions, said George W. Bush.

I didn't make any exceptions, said God.
But you're against evil, aren't you? asked Osama bin Laden.
You are against evil, aren't you? also asked George W. Bush.

I am against evil, said God.
Well, so am I, said Osama bin Laden.
Me too, said George W. Bush.

Killing is evil, said God.
I thought it was necessary in a good cause, said Osama bin Laden.
I also thought it was necessary in a good cause, said George W. Bush.

You cannot fight evil with evil, said God.
Then what am I to do? asked Osama bin Laden.
What am I to do also? asked George W. Bush.

Thou shalt not kill, said God.
I think you're out of touch, said Osama bin Laden.
I'm afraid you're out of touch as well, said George W. Bush.

IV *The New Traffic Rules*

All the Pleasures

I look at clouds. I look at grass. I look at faces. I look at displays in shop windows. I look at the sun rising and the sun setting.

I wake up. I exchange greetings. I do ablutions. I dress. I eat. I walk. I read. I write. I converse. I listen to music. I sleep. Voices speak and pictures come and go.

I wonder at the mysterious and the sublime. I wonder at endless space and endless time. I wonder about existence and non-existence. I wonder about wondering.

On the Fate of Poems

Poems are delicate and easily injured.

During gestation they are particularly vulnerable.

Many are stillborn.

They need care in their early years.

The lucky ones grow robust in the company of others.

A few survive into old age.

By the second generation almost all are forgotten.

A very few are remembered after the exact circumstances of their birth and life are forgotten.

On Death

It does seem like a waste for people to go through childhood, learn a lot, get experience, maybe get some wisdom, and then die.

You say we don't know what happens after we die? Then wasn't it bad planning to torment people with that question? Why not lay out the whole plan before us? We have brains, after all, we have the ability to understand grand schemes, so what's the big secret?

We're not entitled to know the answer? We're not ready to know? Then I go back to my original point. Why aren't we entitled to know? Why aren't we ready? That looks like bad planning to me.

Then we have accidental deaths, deaths by disease, deaths by war. Why go to the trouble of creating intelligent, sensitive people and then torment them? It appears, on the face of it, like a divine screw-up. But I'm ready to be enlightened if somebody can explain it without resorting to far-fetched tales that no sane person can believe unless he's been brainwashed at too early an age to tell an explanation from a hairball of pious fluff.

The Self

Do you not know me?
Do you not recognize me?
Do you not affiliate with me?

I am thy darkness and thy light.
I am thy coming and thy going.
I am thy friend and thy enemy.
I am thy quick particularity searching for a way out.

Maybe in the distant future.
Maybe not in the distant future.

We do not say exactly the word we want to say.
We say the word we are forced to say.
We do not always know the difference.

We persevere along dim passages.

Poetry

It's as if God said –
And now for something different

I feel like an electron
that jumped to another orbit

I was struck by lightning
It didn't kill me
It woke me up

The Right Word

The right word –

Like lightning

Like the crack of a rifle

Like a balm in Gilead

Go to the Dogs

If dogs can be domesticated,
why not people?

If dogs can learn not to bite anybody,
why not people?

If dogs don't do stupid things like risk atomic or
environmental annihilation,
why can't people be more like dogs?

The Life of a Snowflake

I looked out the window
and saw a thousand snowflakes falling
dazzling in their ephemeral existence

One snowflake mused
I'll probably live a normal span
a few moments
but is there life after melting

The snowflake god replied
your constituent parts will join the earth
and so transformed
you'll live forever

Survival Manual

Question everything you're told.

Get someone to watch your back.

Stand up if you don't want to be torn down.

Weather Report to Walt Whitman

The Democratic Vistas are cloudy today

Stormy weather tomorrow

Possible clearing on Friday

The New Traffic Rules

Drachten, The Netherlands.

Hans Monderman, the traffic engineer, has removed all the stop lights, signs, and road markings from the center of town. Even the sidewalks are gone. The intersection at the center of town is a bare brick square.

Cars slow down. Pedestrians go first. Mutual accommodation is the rule. The invisible hand of courtesy and civility is the guide.

"Who has the right of way? I don't care. People here have found their own way, negotiate for themselves, use their own brains."

Grandma crosses the street. The cars stop for her. No one honks, no one shouts. Drivers stop looking at signs, start looking at people. The intersection is "shared space." Cars and pedestrians are equal. In shared space you present yourself as a civil person.

Thanks, Hans Monderman.

Here's what we're going to do. We're going to regard the whole world as shared space. The invisible hand of civility and courtesy will guide us. We're going to accommodate other people in that space. We're going to be civil and courteous to poor people and help them out. We're going to apply the same attitude toward our neighbors in the world. We're going to use "psychological traffic calming" in our relationships with others. The drivers are going to stop running over pedestrians. New traffic rules will be in effect.

V *Earlier Drafts*

Earlier Drafts

In the beginning, God created the heaven and the earth
and then had the uneasy feeling that something had gone
terribly wrong.

She gave me the apple and made me eat it.

Thou shalt not kill unless otherwise instructed.

To exist or not to exist: I can't make up my mind.

To thine own self be true, then it follows thou canst be false?
Canst not be false? It doesn't matter?

Beware the ideas of Marcus Aurelius.

It is a truth universally acknowledged, that a single man
in possession of a good fortune, must be in want of a large
country estate.

The times were pretty good, and at the same time they were
pretty bad.

Happy families are all alike; every unhappy family is a
unique mess.

Oh, say can you see, when the sun is just about to rise, what
so proudly we hailed, when the sun was just about to set last
night?

"Hope" is the thing with hair? fur? skin? an integument? a shell? nothing on? feathers? –

Workers of the world, get your act together. What do you have to lose?

Eighty-seven years ago, our great-grandfathers started a new country with liberty and equality high on their list of priorities.

Alice walked into the looking glass and had to put an ice pack on her forehead.

$E=mc^3$.

The theory of comparativity? Observativity? Standpointivity? How things look from different places?

God does not play canasta.

Sometimes a cigar is just an import from Havana.

Good morning. My name is Ishmael.

As Gregor Samsa awoke one morning from uneasy dreams he found himself transformed in his bed into a gigantic elephant.

To the Tavern? To the Pub? To the Library? To the Grocery Store? To the Circus? To the Movies? To the Lighthouse?

We have nothing to fear but Bankruptcy? Starvation?
Destitution?

Two roads diverged in a wood, and I – had no idea which
one to take.

Is there anything lovely as a tree except perhaps a gorgeous
hunk or a winsome maid?

Candy is dandy but liquor upsets my stomach.

Heroin-cola? Morphine-Cola? Pot-Cola? Cocaine-Cola?

Rubies are a girl's best friend? How about sapphires?
Emeralds? Pearls? Why don't we ask some girls and see what
they say?

Intelligent Design

The children remain unenlightened.
Doesn't that leave you frightened?

The teachers' teaching is phony.
The kids suspect it's baloney.

The nose was designed for glasses.
They teach you that in the classes.

The backside was designed for sitting.
It also serves for shitting.

You must keep your breast under cover
Never to be touched by a lover.

The penis on the statue is missing.
The church forgot about pissing.

The Big Guy thinks it's vain
Ever to use your brain.

It's so decided by the Sages.
Don't mess with the Middle Ages.

Song of Those Who Couldn't Decide

Everyman and Everywoman sat on a wall.

Everyman and Everywoman had a great fall.

All the king's horses and all the king's men

Couldn't put Everyman and Everywoman together again.

Georgie Porgie

Georgie Porgie pudding and pie
Kissed the girls and made them cry.

When the boys came out to play
Georgie Porgie turned savage and killed them.

Ring Around a Rosey

Ring around a rosey

A pocket full of posies

Ashes, ashes

We'll all fall down if we don't verify that they're
actually posies

Too Late to Reconsider

This is killing me, he thought, as he dug his own grave.

Posing for Others to See

Theatrical performances are exactly posed. Even spontaneity in theatrical performances is posed. In life nothing is posed.

I have a button that says, "Life is not a dress rehearsal." I beg to differ. Life is only a dress rehearsal. We never get it right enough to put on the play to our satisfaction.

In a good performance, everything is perfectly posed. In life nothing is perfectly posed.

But aren't we all posing in life? That's right. We are presenting ourselves according to unwritten rules. Each day is a definitive performance, whereas actors continue to perfect their lines.

I got it wrong. What I have written is wrong. Theatrical performances are revised. Life is never revised. Life is not a dress rehearsal.

God Looked Down

God looked down and said
While my back was turned
You've made an unholy mess.

I promised a rainbow next time
You won't be here to see it.

The devil looked up and said
While my back was turned
You've done things I envy.

Never mind the rainbow
You'll feel at home below.

What If We Had Thought Otherwise?

It was necessary –

>to go to war in 1914

>to challenge Russia

>to beggar Germany

>to wait and see what Hitler would do

>to bomb cities in Germany and Japan

>to confront Stalin

>to fight in Vietnam

>to destroy Iraq

>to torture prisoners

>to kill in order to liberate

What if we had thought otherwise?

If Leaders Had Been Wiser: An Exercise in Virtual History

If leaders had been wiser –

there would have been no World War I

there would have been no Bolshevik Revolution

there would have been no Hitler

there would have been no World War II

there would have been no atomic bombs

there would have been no poverty

there would have been no terrorism

there would have been no war-torn planet

there would have been some thought given to the
consequences of decisions made and actions taken

VI *The Wrong House*

The Eyeball

Above all I am not concerned with Poetry.
My subject is War.

        Wilfred Owen

Their heads were targets sticking above the armor.
Their Humvee armor was home-made junk.
They were blasted by shrapnel from C-4 explosives.
Ten marines had their brains blown out.
They jumped to the road and began to return fire.
They jumped to the road and began to return fire.

Then the marines were blasted by grenades.
Arms and legs lay scattered on the road.
Heads and torsos as well as an eye.
The captain ordered the eye to observe
and see where the fire was coming from.
He ordered a finger attached to a trigger
to pull the trigger and return the fire.
To pull the trigger and return the fire.

But the eye was turned in the wrong direction.
He ordered the hand to turn around the eye.
But the hand was too dazed to follow his orders.
The captain directed the leg to kick the hand.
The hand came to and turned around the eye.
The hand came to and turned around the eye.
The captain asked, where the hell shall we shoot?
The eye looked at the target and the finger pulled the trigger.

Soon the finger was blown to bits
and the fighting had to come to a halt.
The medics arrived and swept up the pieces
and sent them to Walter Reed Medical Center.
And sent them to Walter Reed Medical Center.
Some of the arms and legs and heads
were too far gone to make the trip.
They were gently dropped into body bags.
They were gently dropped into body bags.

But the eye survived. Its name was Frank.
The eye was depressed and the eye was angry.
What kind of life could he have as an eye?
But then his eyelid turned up at the hospital
and was grafted back onto his eye.

All trauma patients under the nurse in charge
rage in the ward in desperate anger.
The arms and legs and the hands and heads
raged in the ward in desperate anger
trying to put their lives back together.
Trying to put their lives back together.
What kind of life can we live
as arms and legs and hands and heads?
We aren't ourselves anymore.

Then Stella came into the ward,
another eye that was scraped off the road.
Frank and Stella looked eye to eye.
Frank and Stella became friends and lovers.
They spoke to each other in an unknown code.
They spoke to each other in an unknown code.
Then they were married in the Walter Reed chapel.

Frank the Eye monitored in a bank.
Jorge the Arm turned nuts on bolts.
Sam the Leg got a job as a bouncer.
Bill the Head watched out for terrorists.
Lucille the Torso worked as a model.
Bruno the Hand worked sorting diamonds.

But Stella was unhappy, she wanted a child.
By a stroke of good fortune the medics had found
the sperm and eggs of Frank and Stella
the sperm and eggs of Frank and Stella
spilled on the highway outside of Ramadi.
They vacuumed them up and put them on ice
and sent them to Walter Reed Medical Center.
They were put in a dish and there were united.
A surrogate was found to carry the child.

Who says wars don't have happy endings?
But the captain was kicked out of the Marines.
He let his men down in their time of need.

They were put in a dish and there united.
Who says wars don't have happy endings?

Piss on It

Based on reports that American soldiers urinated on and otherwise desecrated the Koran.

Piss on the Koran

Piss on the Torah

Piss on those who don't read the Bible the way
I read the Bible

Piss on Thou Shalt Not Kill

Piss on Love Thy Neighbor as Thyself

Piss on Do Not Veil the Truth with Falsehood

Piss on prisoners of war

Piss on torture

Piss on rendition

Piss on ragheads

Piss on Baghdad

Piss on Kabul

Piss on the Russians and the Chinese

Piss on the Germans, the French, and the Italians

Piss on genocide in Darfur

Piss on international treaties

Piss on the poor

Piss on the sick

Piss on the starving

Piss on anyone who can't make it

Piss on social security

Piss on anyone who doesn't think the way I think

Piss on anything that I've forgotten to include that should
be pissed on

The Whoosh of a Perfect Shot

A meditation on two M.P.s, both women,
both basketball stars, both who lost their dominant
arms and hands.

I'm playing basketball in my dreams.
I feel the whoosh of a perfect shot.

I wake up and realize my arm is gone.
I lost the whoosh of a perfect shot.

I'm back in Iraq in my dreams.
I hear the whoosh of a grenade.

I wake up and realize my arm is gone.
I lost the whoosh of a perfect shot.

I'm playing basketball again in my dreams.
I feel the whoosh of a perfect shot.

Asleep or awake I'm two different women.
My life has been split apart.

I wish that I could be whole once again
and feel the whoosh of a perfect shot.

The Wrong House

I meet with other mothers. My son is a marine. I'm against
the war. But I'm for my son. I meet with other mothers whose
sons are marines. We don't talk about politics. We talk about
our sons.

I watch TV at three in the morning for names, I'm too unquiet
to sleep. I search the web for news, not about battles,
but about who was killed.

I ask on the phone, how are you, do you need anything, did
you get the package, but I don't ask where are you and what
are you doing, and he doesn't tell me because he doesn't
want me to know and I don't want to know.

I hear the DoD announce a name and I think, thank God
he wasn't mine, and then I reproach myself.

The war has been over several times, and we are freeing
twenty-five million people several times, and we don't talk
about it.

We all fear two marines coming down the front walk, it's an
image that we avoid, but we can't avoid it.

The day came, I saw two marines coming down the front
walk, my back was turned, I saw them reflected in the mirror.

They're coming to the wrong house! I'm sure they're coming
to the wrong house! I'm sure they're coming to the wrong
house!

My hand is on his coffin, my head is on his coffin, the earth is on his coffin, hands reach out to me, hands touch me, hands comfort me, but they cannot reach me, they cannot touch me, they cannot comfort me.

Thank you, thank you. Your hands cannot reach me. They cannot touch me. They cannot comfort me. It is of little use. It is of little use. I rewind time. It is of little use. I am on a far shore alone. I am on a far shore alone.

The Helpless Giant

He celebrates himself.
He invites his soul.
Men and women are as good as he is and are at his side.
He sings and dances among them and children join in and
are not afraid.

He and they possess the earth and the skies.
He luxuriates on the grass. In the evening there is a great heat
in the fire and he and they warm themselves before it.

He climbs mountains with ease and swims rivers with ease.
He strides across continents with ease.
He cultivates farms, builds cities, and shouts a great shout
around the globe.

He lifts up the poor and the sick and gives a home to teeming
masses.
He walks with free men and free women and former slaves
who are now as free.
He reads books and recites poems and with his hands makes
marvelous devices.

He goes to war in the company of men, he is present in the
company of women who do the work at home, he defeats a
savage enemy and then he and they rebuild war-torn lands.

Time passes and he goes into the jungle, deeper into the
jungle, into the darkness.

His feet are caught in tangled vines and his right arm is caught in tangled vines and the stench of the jungle sickens him. He swings with his free hand and savagely kills, rabbits, lions, deer.

Vines tangle him and snakes mar his body and the venom sickens him.

Wild birds gall and bloody his face.

His feet sink into marshes and they engulf him.

He spends his power. He cannot move. He cannot move in and he cannot move out. He bears blindness and pain and scorn.

Once he reached the clouds and wore robes of gold and silk and doffed them for homespun cloth when at his ease.

Once men and women came around to sing and dance and children came near and now they are afraid.

Once he possessed the earth and skies and luxuriated on the grass and celebrated himself. No longer.

He does not climb mountains nor swim rivers nor shout a lusty shout.

He does not wear robes of gold and silk and commune with men and women and come near children.

He cannot take his ease unless the darkness lifts and sight returns to his eyes.

He cannot take his ease unless the swoon passes and he remembers himself and recognizes himself and accepts himself and celebrates himself and invites his soul once again.

VII *Casualties of War: Stories*

The Glorious Life of Lieutenant Case

The President sat with his boots propped up on the desk in the Oval Office, somewhere between somnolence and waking. Colonel Sands stood on the far side of the desk reading aloud from a classified document. The left side of his mouth quivered from time to time.

The President dozed until Sands read " . . . on this secret mission in Iraq we have assigned Captain Anthony Jones, Lieutenant Robert Sanford, Lieutenant Ricardo Gonzalez, and just in case, . . . "

"Hold it, Sandy. What's Justin Case's rank?"

"Mr. President, I, hmm . . . that's not . . . hmm . . . "

"Goddamn it, Sandy, just answer the question." His mouth turned into a downward curving arc.

"I . . . I'll have to, hmm, get back to you, ya know, on this one." The left side of his mouth quivered.

"Get on a secure line and get me a goddamn answer."

Sands got on a secure line. The Assistant Secretary of Defense for Middle Eastern Affairs was speaking.

"How do I know what to say? Ask Rummy."

Rummy pursed his lips when he got the call. "Look. Give the president what he wants. Don't get me hung up on trivia, for Christ's sake."

"That's Lieutenant Justin Case, Mr. President."

"Who is he? What's his background? What'd he do to get on this mission? I want a full report, Sandy, and I want it now."

"I'm sorry to bother you again, Mr. Secretary." Back on the secure line. "The President wants a full report on Justin Case."

The Secretary pursed his lips again. "You'd better call Dick. Let him finesse this one. I'm out of it."

The Vice President mouth turned into an asymmetrical scowl. "We can't go back now, Sands. You'll have to give Case a background. You'll have to give him some exploits. You don't get to go on a secret mission just for being alive.

"Give him parents who live in New York. People don't know their next door neighbors there. Give him a dog named Squat. Give him a Medal of Honor. He wiped out a whole mosque-full of insurgents in Falluja. Give him shrapnel in his leg. Give him a great sense of *joie de vivre*. What the hell, Sands, write a story."

Sands returned to the Oval Office with an official record on Lieutenant Justin Case.

"I want to meet Case. Bring him here."

"But Mr. President, he's in Iraq as we speak." Sands' tic bothered him dreadfully. The President didn't notice.

"Look, I'm the President of the goddamn United States and leader of the goddamn free world. Bring me Lieutenant Justin Case on the next plane."

Back to the secure line with the V.P.

"We've got to turn Case into a national hero, that's what we've got to do, Sands. Case is on a secret mission in Iran now, you got it?"

Back in the Oval Office.

"Mr. President, Lieutenant Justin Case is already on a secret mission in Iran. We can't get him just now."

"All right, Sandy. Stop trembling. The country needs a shot in the arm. Get Karl to write a scenario. When Case gets back, we'll bring him here and tell his story."

Sands to the V.P. on a secure line. "So that's what the President said."

"Yeah. I guess we'll have to get Justin Case killed and bring him back in a coffin and give him a funeral at Arlington. The public will get a lift. You better line up some parents named Case. From New York."

Sands gave the President the sad news that Case was coming home in a coffin. The President went to Arlington for the parade, honor guard, flag-draped coffin, taps. The elder Cases were handed the flag and a check for $12,000. The President was somber. The nation was uplifted.

Moses' Nail Clipping

I'm the custodian in the state court in Alabama and among my duties is looking after a glass case in the rotunda with Moses' nail clipping in it.

I'm just a custodian, but this line of work goes back three generations. I'm now sixty-two, and I got a wife and two grown kids, a girl and a boy. I been working this job about thirty-three years.

I know Moses' nail clipping is a piece of history like you find in a museum. Folks come from all around to see it. The judge set it up here in a glass case. I hear that Moses snagged a nail when he was holding the Ten Commandments and he had to clip it. Somehow this clipping found its way to the judge's courthouse in Alabama. The judge is very proud to have the possession of it.

Then some people got the idea that Moses' nail clipping had no business in a court of law. What ideas some people get makes me wonder at their sanity. I myself see no harm having Moses' nail clipping here. But these folks alleged Moses' nail clipping was a religious object, and it had no business being in a law court, which is a secular institution.

Well, these folks went all the way up to the Supreme Court in Washington, D.C. They were saying, what about a cross on top of the courthouse, or a Jewish star, or whatever the Arabs have? Were these proper objects for a courthouse? How Moses' nail clipping got mixed in with all that, I don't know.

Well, Jesus Christ, if you pardon me saying so, I just take care of Moses' nail clipping and stay out of politics.

The fact is, when I was cleaning around once some while back and had the glass case off, Moses' nail clipping blew away somewhere and I could not find it for the life of me. So what did I do? Well, let me tell you. I clipped my own nail the exact same size and shape and put it in the case and nobody detected the difference or made a fuss or did anything whatsoever.

Casualties of War

Frank Anderson was killed outside of Tikrit in June. He went from the football field to the battlefield and then he died.

We met at the Anderson's house a week after the news came.

I knew Frank as his high school football coach. He was a good athlete with a talent for football. He did drugs a little. He drank a little. It's typical. It's ordinary. I let these issues pass.

He wanted to join the Marines. My comments were pointless. He graduated and then signed up. He followed a family tradition: Grandfather, father, son. Second World War, Vietnam, Iraq. He had an image ingrained in him that he had to live up to: All-American Boy. He never knew who he was. He didn't live long enough to find out.

I believe he thought of the Marines as an extension of the football team, except when you're tackled in football, you get up and go home. The Marines were sort of a great big football team that played away games. And he was on the winning team.

The one time he came back on leave, he had an argument with his best friend. "If I'm ordered to shoot, I will have no hesitation." They had to drop the subject.

The Andersons put up a brave front. They had thirty or thirty-five relatives and friends come over a week after they heard the news. They had to act as if this was a kind of ceremony. It *was* a kind of ceremony.

George got up to speak. That's Frank's father. He held up a picture of Frank in his Marine Corps uniform and he looked like he was saying, here's what I gave up, but his words didn't come out that way and he said something different, I guess what he thought he ought to say.

"Maria and I are patriots." He paused between all these comments. "We passed on our pride to Frank." Pause. "We always wanted him to be somebody. Now he is." Pause. "He had a mission and his mission is accomplished. He did what he thought was right." Pause. "I'm proud. I'm not sorry."

He hesitated. He tried to control his demeanor, but he looked dazed or stupefied.

"They gave him the Medal of Honor. I want you to see it."

That statement surprised me because none of us had heard about a medal.

He went upstairs.

I looked at Maria and fear spread across her face. The fear spread to me and I asked her what was going on.

"There is no medal. Frank was fooling around with his gun. He thought the clip was empty. But it wasn't. He killed himself. George can't face it. You'd better go look after him."

At that moment we heard a loud bang. Conversation stopped instantly. I rushed upstairs. I yelled down, "Somebody call an ambulance. George has shot himself."

References

The pieces in this book were written between December 2004 and June 2005. Specific information is based on published accounts.

1. The Capacious Tent, p. 7. On December 21, 2004, a suicide bomber entered a mess tent at a US military base outside of Mosul and killed 22 American soldiers and support staff, and wounded 60 others.

2. The President Delivers His Second Inaugural Address, p. 10. The plight of the world's children is documented in *The State of the World's Children 2005: Childhood Under Threat*, published by UNICEF, December 2004.

3. Eight Days in Falluja, p. 15. My account is based on a report by Dexter Filkins that appeared in *The New York Times*, November 21, 2004.

4. Never Again, p. 44. On February 4, 2005, *The New York Times* reported that Marine Corps Lt. Gen. James N. Mattis, who commanded US forces in Afghanistan and Iraq, remarked at a meeting in San Diego, "Actually, it's a lot of fun to fight. You know, it's a hell of a hoot. It's fun to shoot some people. I'll be right upfront with you, I like brawling." He added: "You know, guys like that [in Afghanistan "who slap women around . . . because they didn't wear a veil"] ain't got no manhood left anyway. So it's a hell of a lot of fun to shoot them." The general subsequently agreed that he should have chosen his words more carefully.

5. The New Traffic Rules, p. 65. My comment is based on an article in *The New York Times*, January 22, 2005, entitled "A Path To Road Safety With No Signposts," written by Sarah Lyall.

6. The Whoosh of a Perfect Shot, p. 88. This poem derives from a lengthy article in *The New York Times*, April 10, 2005, by Juliet Mancur, entitled "Two Women, Bound by Sports, War, and Injuries." See page 105 of the Postscript for further comments on this piece and on The Eyeball.

7. The Wrong House, p. 89. This elegy is partly based on observations made by Cynthia Gorney in "A Mothers' War," *The New York Times Magazine*, May 29, 2005.

Postscript

It is so easy to be misunderstood that I want to explain what I have written before anybody else does.

The Twin Towers

Every time that I see a panoramic view of Manhattan, in pictures or on television or in the movies, I involuntarily look for the Twin Towers, knowing that if the picture was made before September 11, 2001, I will see them, and if it was made after September 11, 2001, I will not. Then I gaze into nowhere and feel my post-traumatic stress disorder come over me. This is probably a very common experience for Americans, and it is the only legacy of Al Qaeda aside from all the bloodshed: They will never change the United States in any fundamental way. They wanted to make the point that the United States is evil and vulnerable, but instead, they made the opposite point and caused most of the world to rally around us.

This much I have said in "The Twin Towers." But then George W. Bush, in a very confused way, struck at the wrong enemy at the cost of many more lives than was necessary to pursue Al Qaeda.

Nightmares

The fury expressed in "Nightmares" is not that of "twins," which is merely a literary device, but of half of America. The other half has been disoriented by patriotic hallucinations, which clear up as the casualties mount.

Elegy for American Soldiers Killed in Iraq

The names in the "Elegy for American Soldiers Killed in Iraq" are the names of those who once were very young, real living people who deserve some thought about who they might have become if their lives had not been stupidly wasted, and some thought about the terminal loss that they suffered because of someone else's power to indulge his delusions with their lives.

I Saw This

"I Saw This" is in some way a testament concerning my own life because I have lived in the narrow spaces between the horrors of genocide, war, and misery, through no virtue of mine, but by mere chance. In watching all these horrors along with others, I believe that the revulsion that we feel, easily communicated throughout the world now through television, the Internet, and cell phones, will eventually coalesce into a force, never known in the world before, to create real civilization for the first time. I do not know how long it will take for power to shift to those who until now have been dispersed and powerless, but the conditions already exist.

Two Conversations and Thou Shalt Not Kill

In "Two Conversations" and "Thou Shalt Not Kill," I deal with the absurdity of enemies, each of whom hears the voice of God telling him to do injury to the other. Those who claim to be guided by the voice of God have a terrifying justification for doing anything, no matter how outrageous or self-destructive. We should hunt down terrorists, not because God tells us to, but because they are murderers. We should refrain from preemptive war, not because God tells us to, but because the evidence is fabricated. After so many disasters perpetrated in the name of God, my considered advice is to deal with God directly rather than through intermediaries. When God tells us to be nasty to our neighbors, I would get a second opinion.

The Eyeball and The Whoosh of a Perfect Shot

I wrote "The Eyeball" and "The Whoosh of a Perfect Shot" after reading two stories in *The New York Times*. The first, on April 25, 2005, describes the battering of 185 marines in Company E, of whom more than one-third were killed or wounded, quite a few in jerry-rigged Humvees. The second, on April 10, 2005, is a detailed account about two female M.P.s, one white and one black, both college basketball stars, who aspired to become professionals. Both had their dominant hands and arms blown off in Iraq and saw their lives spin out of control. They met at Walter Reed Medical Center and supported each other in trying to make peace with their traumas.

The body parts in "The Eyeball" are stand-ins for damaged bodies that the wounded have to live with for the rest of their lives. More than that, I mean the depiction of the grotesquely impossible, living body parts, as a damnation of war and so-called statesmen intoxicated with war. My message is that war is madness and this one is unnecessary, but somehow we can't produce the few hundred or the few thousand well-armored Humvees needed – I don't know which number is correct – but during the Second World War we were able to produce over 300,000 planes and 86,000 tanks, and Humvees aren't even tanks.

I have tried to evoke the wistfulness of each young woman, conveyed in the *Times* article, in "The Whoosh of a Perfect Shot," and surely the wistfulness and despair of any man, woman, or child disabled by war. It is foolish to think that any war is just. No war rises above the level of "necessary."

The Helpless Giant

The final poem in this collection celebrates America as a land of limitless possibilities in the manner of Walt Whitman. I truncate history and allude to The Second World War. Then I describe the giant as helplessly mired in Iraq — it could be Vietnam as well. I use the impenetrable jungle as a metaphor. Then I end with the proposition that America can some day be America again.

* * * *

The Noble Duke of York

I placed the nursery rhyme, "The Noble Duke of York," at the beginning of this book because it epitomizes the absurdity of empty military gestures, except that the Duke of York was not trying to frighten the entire world into submission.

Virtual Reality

Virtual reality refers to what might have happened in the past had different decisions been made. I will forego that exercise and imagine what might happen in the future.

The war in Iraq will wind down, some kind of resolution will take place there, the world will remain about the same as it was before, the dead will remain dead and the maimed will remain maimed. A US government will eventually come along and pick up the pieces. It will revert to cooperation with allies, it will honor international treaties, it will help to alleviate world poverty, it will avoid war in favor of diplomacy, and it will build a new monument for mourners to go and mourn.

I hope that these explanations are sufficient to clarify everything in this book.

Photo by Liz Sharpe

Mike Sharpe has written widely on economics, politics, and world affairs, and is the author of *John Kenneth Galbraith and the Lower Economics*. He worked with Senators Humphrey and Javits to draft The Full Employment and Balanced Growth Act of 1978 and was economic advisor to Senator Birch Bayh in his bid for the presidency. He is founder and president of M. E. Sharpe publishing company.